Satan Swallowed Up

For My Parents
Louis and Evelyn Goldstein
My daughter, Maria
My granddaughters Sarina & Juliette

Copyright © 2015 by Living Epistles Ministries
All rights reserved under International Copyright Law.
2nd Edition
Published @ Long Island, NY February, 2015

ISBN: 13: 978-0692261514
ISBN: 10: 0692261516

Satan Swallowed Up
Sheila R. Vitale

No part of this book may be reproduced, in any form, without written permission from the publisher

Requests for permission to reproduce selections from this book should be mailed to:

Living Epistles Ministries
Sheila R. Vitale
P O Box 562
Port Jefferson Station, NY 11776-0562 USA
(631) 331-1493

Living Epistles Ministries

Sheila R. Vitale
Pastor, Teacher, Founder
PO Box 562
Port Jefferson Station, NY 11776 USA

SATAN SWALLOWED UP

Is an Edited Transcript of LEM Message #005

Satan Swallowed Up

Transcribed and Edited For Clarity,
Continuity of Thought, and Punctuation by
The LEM Transcribing and Editing Team

Formatted As a Book by
The LEM Professional Administrators Staff

Living Epistles Ministries
~ Judeo-Christian Spiritual Philosophy ~
Sheila R. Vitale
Pastor, Teacher & Founder

Ministry Staff
Anthony Milton, Teacher (South Carolina)
Brooke Paige, Teacher (New York)
Sandra Aldrich (MN) (July 7, 1975 – April 18, 2021)

Administrative Staff
Susan Panebianco, Office Manager

Editorial Staff
Rose Herczeg, Editor

Technical Staff
Lape Mobolaji-Lawal, Database Administrator

Ministry Illustrators
Cecilia H. Bryant (Oct. 18, 1921 – Oct. 23, 2013)
Fidelis Onwubueke

Music Staff
June Eble, Singer, Lyricist and Clarinetist
(July 20, 1931 – Jan. 24, 2024)
Don Gervais, Singer, Lyricist and Guitarist
Rita L. Rora, Singer, Lyricist and Guitarist

Table of Contents

ALTERNATE TRANSLATIONS IN THIS BOOK 1
PROPHECY II
THE FIRST ADAM 1
    A GREAT WONDER IN HEAVEN A SPIRITUAL SIGN 3
    THE SUN, MOON & STARS 4
    A PAINFUL PROCESS 5
    BRINGING EMOTIONS INTO SUBMISSION 6
    CROWNS 7
    STARS 7
    THE NUMBER TWELVE 8
    CHRIST IN US, OUR DAILY SACRIFICE 8
    THE ORDER OF THE KINGDOM 9
    TWO ANOINTINGS 10
        The Imputed Anointing 10
        The Imparted Anointing 11
        Transitioning Into Christ 12
SATAN'S KINGDOM IS ENDING 13
    THE CARNAL MIND UNDERNEATH THE CHRIST MIND 14
    PREGNANT WITH THE CHRIST CHILD 15
    THE PURPOSE OF TRIALS 16
    THE DRAGON 18
    OUT OF ORDER 20
    A FALSE ANOINTING 20
    DECEPTION AND SEDUCTION 21
    ONE SPIRITUAL CREATION 24
    THE SON ABIDES FOREVER 25
    SOUL MAN TO SPIRITUAL MAN 26
    BRINGING FORTH THE HOLY CHILD 28
    RULING BY THE INDWELLING CHRIST 29
CHRIST OVERCOMING IN US 31
    THE LAW OF MOSES 31
    THE LAW IS SPIRITUAL 31

THE LAW IS CONTRARY TO HUMAN NATURE	32
CHRIST JESUS, THE FULFILLMENT OF THE LAW	33
THREE TRIMESTERS	38
CHRIST TRIUMPHANT	39
PROPHECY	**41**
TABLE OF REFERENCES	**43**
ABOUT THE AUTHOR	**45**

The Alternate Translation Bible©

***The Alternate Translation Bible* (ATB)** is an original translation of the Scripture.

Alternate Translation of the Old Testament©
Alternate Translation, Exodus, Chapter 32
    (Crime of the Calf)©
Alternate Translation, Daniel, Chapter 8©
Alternate Translation, Daniel, Chapter 11©

Alternate Translation of the New Testament©
Alternate Translation, 2 Thessalonians, Chapter 2
    (Sophia)©
Alternate Translation, 1st John, Chapter 5©
Alternate Translation, the Book of Colossians
    (To The Church At Colosse) ©
Alternate Translation, the Book of Corinthians, Chapter 11
    (Corinthian Confusion) ©
Alternate Translation, the Book of Jude
    (The Common Salvation)©

Alternate Translation of the Book of the Revelation of Jesus Christ to St. John©
Traducción Alternada del Libro de Revelación de Jesucristo©

ALTERNATE TRANSLATIONS IN THIS BOOK

REV 12:1 – AT 15

Satan Swallowed Up

PROPHECY

(By Disciple)

Thus saith the Spirit of the Living God, for I indeed seek for those who worship me in spirit and in truth, and if man would just step back, I shall step in and overtake. I shall rule and rule here, and rule the services, I shall be all in all. I shall speak unto my people, and I say unto you, continue to yield your members to me and I shall pour blessings, and anointing, and ministry that thou hast not known before. Continue to step back, and I shall give thee all the things that I have promised in my Word. It shall begin to come to pass, saith the Living God, for indeed I am looking for those who will worship me in spirit and in truth, and I shall begin to reveal to you what that truly means, saith God. Listen to my Word that is coming forth, harken unto my Word that will be spoken through my prophet this day, for it indeed shall bring life unto you. It shall quicken your spirit, and it shall continue to make you into my image, saith God, for I shall speak and I shall speak this day. Listen and ask me for understanding, and it shall mean life unto your bones, saith God. Hallelujah.

THE FIRST ADAM

Jehovah formed Adam (mankind) from the dust, and he became a living, or an immortal, soul (Gen. 2:7); but he sinned (Gen 3:11) and then he died (Gen 5:5). It is a great mystery, but the First Man (1 Cor. 15:47), or the First Adam, that living soul that died, is the soul that lives on the inside of the material bodies of humanity.

The Second Man, or the Second Adam, is Christ Jesus, the lord from heaven (1 Cor. 15:47). He is the holy soul (as opposed to the fallen soul of the First Man) that can relate to both God and man, and the only soul by which the First Man (Adam) can have a relationship with Jehovah (1 Tim. 2:5).

Christ Jesus, the Second Adam (as well as the First Adam), lives on the inside of the material bodies of humanity. Their relationship can be likened to the relationship between Cain and Abel (Gen. 4:7). Righteous Adam, is born again as Christ Jesus, our New Man (Col 3:10), for the specific purpose of destroying his own murderer (Jn 8:44).

Rev 12:1-5

[1] AND THERE APPEARED A GREAT WONDER IN HEAVEN; A WOMAN CLOTHED WITH THE SUN, AND THE MOON UNDER HER FEET, AND UPON HER HEAD A CROWN OF TWELVE STARS:

[2] AND SHE BEING WITH CHILD CRIED, TRAVAILING IN BIRTH, AND PAINED TO BE DELIVERED.

[3] AND THERE APPEARED ANOTHER WONDER IN HEAVEN; AND BEHOLD A GREAT RED DRAGON, HAVING SEVEN HEADS AND TEN HORNS, AND SEVEN CROWNS UPON HIS HEADS.

[4] AND HIS TAIL DREW THE THIRD PART OF THE STARS OF HEAVEN, AND DID CAST THEM TO THE EARTH: AND THE

DRAGON STOOD BEFORE THE WOMAN WHICH WAS READY TO BE DELIVERED, FOR TO DEVOUR HER CHILD AS SOON AS IT WAS BORN.

[5] AND SHE BROUGHT FORTH A MAN CHILD, WHO WAS TO RULE ALL NATIONS WITH A ROD OF IRON: AND HER CHILD WAS CAUGHT UP UNTO GOD, AND TO HIS THRONE. **KJV**

How do we know whether someone has been incarnated or born into this earth world at the express will of the Father, or at the express will of the First Adam? Everyone born with the seed of the Father appears as a natural man who was incarnated at the will of the First Adam, until the holy seed within them matures into the full image of Christ. The characteristics of the man that was birthed at the express will of the First Adam is discussed in previous messages.

Jer 31:27

[27] BEHOLD, THE DAYS COME, SAITH THE LORD, THAT I WILL SOW THE HOUSE OF ISRAEL AND THE HOUSE OF JUDAH WITH THE SEED OF MAN, AND WITH THE SEED OF BEAST. **KJV**

Spiritual truth and wisdom are given to edify us, not to determine who is a good guy and who is a bad guy. We are all members of one soul called "the First Adam," and understand that it is the will of the Lord that all men should be saved.

We do not have the full mind of Jesus Christ right now, so we cannot see how everything will work for the good, but it will, because Jesus is the Son of God. He is not man.

Rev 12:1-4 is about the First Adam. Everyone here, seen from an alternate point of viewpoint, would appear very different.

For example, we can view a man with a child in his arms, as a husband embracing his wife, or as a businessman rebuking one of his employees. But, if someone from the planet Mars (who did not know anything about human beings) saw the same man wearing different clothing each time, he would think they were different men.

Satan Swallowed Up/   The First Adam

In like manner, God is revealing Adam, His creation, from different viewpoints. Rev 12:1-4 is a spiritual description of the First Adam in the process of producing the life of Christ.

A Great Wonder in Heaven
A Spiritual Sign

Rev 12:1

> ¹ AND THERE APPEARED A GREAT WONDER IN HEAVEN.... **KJV**

A great wonder is a spiritual sign. The word *heavens* does not describe the blue sky above. It refers to the spiritual world. There is the earth world, which relates to the body, and the spirit world. The soul is a part the spirit world, but lower than heaven where the Lord Jesus Christ is.

Rev 12:1

> ¹ AND THERE APPEARED A GREAT WONDER IN HEAVEN... **KJV**

The woman of Rev 12 is not a woman in a natural body. She is a spiritual woman, and Rev 12:1 is saying that her appearance in heaven is a great spiritual sign.

The entire Scripture is about God, so everything written and everyone written about is spiritual in relation to God. The soul world and the Church are female in relation to God, and the Lord Jesus Christ is marrying the Church.

This spiritual woman is clothed with the sun, and the moon is under her feet. The Greek word translated *sun* means *light, east* and *sun*. The word *sun* throughout the Scripture typifies the Lord, because it means light.

Ps 84:11

> ¹¹ THE LORD GOD IS A SUN AND SHIELD.... **KJV**

Mal 4:2

> ² BUT UNTO YOU THAT FEAR MY NAME, SHALL THE SUN OF RIGHTEOUSNESS ARISE WITH HEALING IN HIS WINGS. . . . **KJV**

She is covered, she is clothed with the sun.

Rev 12:1

> ¹ . . . AND THE MOON UNDER HER FEET. . . . **KJV**

The Greek word translated *woman* means *to generate, to come into being.* This woman is about to marry and produce a spiritual child.

God made two great lights, the greater to rule the day and the lesser to rule the night (Gen 1:16). The sun (Jesus Christ), rules the world of the light, which is the world of the Spirit of God; and the moon rules the world of the night, which is the world of darkness. We live in the world of darkness, which is ruled by the First Adam, before we are saved. This darkness is in man's mind and emotions, which are base.

The Sun, Moon & Stars

Gen 37:9-10

> ⁹ AND HE DREAMED YET ANOTHER DREAM, AND TOLD IT HIS BRETHREN, AND SAID, BEHOLD, I HAVE DREAMED A DREAM MORE; AND, BEHOLD, THE SUN AND THE MOON AND THE ELEVEN STARS MADE OBEISANCE TO ME.
>
> ¹⁰ AND HE TOLD IT TO HIS FATHER, AND TO HIS BRETHREN: AND HIS FATHER REBUKED HIM, AND SAID UNTO HIM, WHAT IS THIS DREAM THAT THOU HAST DREAMED? SHALL I AND THY MOTHER AND THY BRETHREN INDEED COME TO BOW DOWN OURSELVES TO THEE TO THE EARTH? **KJV**

The sun represents the father, the moon represents the mother, and the eleven stars represent the brothers.

Some Scripture can be taken literally. The history, for example, is authentic, but everything in the Book of Revelation is symbolic. The symbols in the Book of Revelation are interpreted by comparing Scripture with Scripture to see how the same symbols are used elsewhere.

Rev 12:1

[1] ... AND THE MOON UNDER HER FEET .... **KJV**

Underfoot means, ***the one who is under spiritual authority.***

Rom 16:20

[20] AND THE GOD OF PEACE SHALL BRUISE SATAN UNDER YOUR FEET SHORTLY. THE GRACE OF OUR LORD JESUS CHRIST BE WITH YOU. AMEN. **KVJ**

Heb 2:6-8

[6] BUT ONE IN A CERTAIN PLACE TESTIFIED, SAYING, WHAT IS MAN, THAT THOU ART MINDFUL OF HIM? OR THE SON OF MAN, THAT THOU VISITEST HIM?

[7] THOU MADEST HIM A LITTLE LOWER THAN THE ANGELS; THOU CROWNEDST HIM WITH GLORY AND HONOUR, AND DIDST SET HIM OVER THE WORKS OF THY HANDS:

[8] THOU HAST PUT ALL THINGS IN SUBJECTION UNDER HIS FEET. FOR IN THAT HE PUT ALL IN SUBJECTION UNDER HIM, HE LEFT NOTHING THAT IS NOT PUT UNDER HIM. BUT NOW WE SEE NOT YET ALL THINGS PUT UNDER HIM. **KJV**

A Painful Process

We appear to be one entity, but are not. There are many elements within us. We are soul (personality), and we are spirit (mind). The elements of the First Adam have been out of order since Adam lost the covering of God (when they were fused together to make one spiritually dead entity), and sometimes unholy fruit is produced from the illegal interactions of his parts.

Jesus Christ is breaking apart the soul of the First Adam for the specific purpose of putting him back together in the proper order, and that breaking apart is a very painful experience. The Scripture likens it in to the plowing of the earth.

Our personality (soul) is attached to the First Adam, who abides in the physical bodies of mortal humanity. The soul is in the body, and the spirit is rooted in the mind. Our spiritual growth can be likened to a plant. Before life can sprout in a man, the Lord Jesus plows the earth that his soul is planted with a spiritual plow, and that is pretty painful.

The farmer plows the earth. He turns it over, and everything that opposes the growth of the seed is rooted out. The weeds and the stones, which typify the elements of the human personality, are rooted out. Sometimes the spiritual weeds and stones take the form of demons, sometimes curses.

There is nothing to be afraid of, because the whole human race is in this condition. Some people are frightened when they hear about curses and demons, but they are not the only one with a spiritual problem. Whether they believe it or not, this is the condition of the whole human race. Jesus Christ came to deliver us from these spiritual problems, so there is nothing to be frightened of. He came to give us a better life in Him.

Bringing Emotions Into Submission

The moon is under her feet. The woman clothed with the sun is the First Adam. She has the authority of God upon her, and the moon, representing the base emotions of man, are under her feet. God is ruling in her, and her emotions are under her feet. These emotions are not going away. Many in deliverance ministry believe that these base emotions can be completely cast out. But I do not believe that. When these base emotions have produced ungodly fruit, that fruit, which is demons, must be cast out. The emotions themselves, which are an inherited part of the First Adam, can only be satisfied by Jesus Christ, and the only path to permanent satisfaction is submission to Him. Satan (who is a party to the spiritual adultery that births the demons) must be driven under the authority of Christ while he continues to perform his function of giving form to the creation.

The woman's emotions are under her feet. They are in the proper position where they can do no harm, but they are still giving form to the creation.

Crowns

Rev 12:1

> [1] ... AND UPON HER HEAD WAS A CROWN OF TWELVE STARS. **KJV**

Crowns in the Scripture represent authority, ruling, the ability and privilege of ruling, and, in some cases, righteousness. Evil powers can wear crowns. There were ungodly kings who wore crowns.

This means that, at the moment they are wearing the crowns they have authority, and authority means power. *Crowns* always represent the power of life and death over of the person that they are ruling.

Stars

Rev 1:20

> [20] ...THE SEVEN STARS ARE THE ANGELS OF THE SEVEN CHURCHES:.... **KJV**

Ps 136:9

> [9] THE MOON AND STARS RULE BY NIGHT, FOR HIS MERCY ENDURETH FOREVER. **KJV**

The stars are given a position of rulership along with the sun and the moon. The sun is ruling the heavenlies, the moon is ruling in the world of the First Adam (which is base darkness), and the stars have spiritual authority. These are the spiritual powers that are upon the head of this woman. The number twelve refers to God's perfect government. Joseph dreamt that his father, mother and his eleven brothers would bow down to him.

The Number Twelve

The number twelve points to the twelve tribes of Israel who bring forth the leadership of God in the earth. In the Old Testament, Israel was the one nation that the government of God rested upon. But in this hour Jesus Christ is bringing forth a spiritual government, which is his Spirit in the people that He chooses.

The twelve stars indicate a spiritual government. There are no identifiable Israelite tribes today. We know only what He tells us because, today, we see through a glass darkly. We know only that the fullness of God's government, symbolized by the number twelve, is in the earth today.

Christ in Us,
Our Daily Sacrifice

Dan 8:11

> [11] YEA, HE MAGNIFIED HIMSELF EVEN TO THE PRINCE OF THE HOST, AND BY HIM THE DAILY SACRIFICE WAS TAKEN AWAY.... **KJV**

The daily sacrifice in the Old Testament was the continuous burning of animal flesh to purge Israel's sins. Today in the New Testament, our daily sacrifice is the presence of the indwelling Christ, our sinless sacrifice; the Lamb that dwells within us that purifies us from sin by burning our sin nature. The sweet savor that Jehovah smells is the spiritual crucifixion of Christ who is nailed to our sin-filled soul.

Christ in us cries to the father to save his soul life, and our soul, which is nailed to his soul, is saved also. We partake of this work of the spiritual cross when we deny out sin nature.

<u>Gal 2:20</u>

> [20] I AM CRUCIFIED WITH CHRIST: NEVERTHELESS I LIVE; YET NOT I, BUT CHRIST LIVETH IN ME: AND THE LIFE WHICH I NOW LIVE IN THE FLESH I LIVE BY THE FAITH OF THE SON OF GOD, WHO LOVED ME, AND GAVE HIMSELF FOR ME. **KJV**

The body is the temple of the Holy Ghost, the sanctuary where the sacrifice takes place. Jesus' body was cast down (died) so that Christ, his seed, could be crucified to our mortal soul (which is likened to wood).

<u>Dan 8:11</u>

> [11] . . . AND THE PLACE OF HIS SANCTUARY WAS CAST DOWN. **KJV**

Antichrist was able to cast down some of the stars of heaven because of transgressions in the government of God. There was error, there was sin in the government of God, so they were cast down to the earth. They were no longer sitting in the heavenlies with God.

<u>Dan 8:12</u>

> [12] .AND AN HOST WAS GIVEN HIM AGAINST THE DAILY SACRIFICE BY REASON OF TRANSGRESSION, .AND IT CAST DOWN THE TRUTH. . . . **KJV**

The stars represent the Truth. The casting down of the stars is the casting down of the truth.

The Order of the Kingdom

<u>Rev 12:1-2</u>

> [1] AND THERE APPEARED A GREAT WONDER IN HEAVEN; A WOMAN CLOTHED WITH THE SUN, AND THE MOON UNDER HER FEET, AND UPON HER HEAD A CROWN OF TWELVE STARS:
>
> [2] AND SHE BEING WITH CHILD CRIED, TRAVAILING IN BIRTH, AND PAINED TO BE DELIVERED. **KJV**

The woman is in the proper order for the government of God to function. Her head is covered, and her emotions are under her feet.

1 Cor 11:3
> [3] BUT I WOULD HAVE YOU KNOW, THAT THE HEAD OF EVERY MAN IS CHRIST; AND THE HEAD OF THE WOMAN IS THE MAN; AND THE HEAD OF CHRIST IS GOD. **KJV**

The sun in this Scripture typifies Christ, the Son of God, and the crown is the Father. The woman is the human spirit of the First Adam, which is attached to the Father and the Son, above. Her emotional soul, represented by the moon, is under her feet. She is clothed with the sun, that is, in perfect spiritual order.

Two Anointings

There are two kinds of anointing: The imputed anointing and the imparted anointing.

The Imputed Anointing

The gifts and calling of God are given without repentance. A preacher can do the great works of God (prophesying, healing, delivering), and be written up in the newspaper the next day for committing a crime that he has not denied. He actually confessed, so we know that it is the truth. ***How could this happen?***

Rom 11:21
> [21] FOR IF GOD SPARED NOT THE NATURAL BRANCHES, TAKE HEED LEST HE ALSO SPARE NOT THEE. **KJV**

God wants his people to hear the Word of God and to be healed and delivered, so He takes an unclensed man and loans him His Spirit. He gives him the power to minister to the people. Most resist the temptations that plague ministers, but sometimes a man falls. Disappointment is understandable, because he was an imperfect man. But anyone who is so disappointed that he loses his faith in God, is guilty of idolatry.

He had the imputed anointing, the loaned authority of God. People who do not understand this, expect their pastors to be perfect, but they are not perfect. Only Christ is perfect. Pastors, and everyone else, will be perfect only when they are fully unified with Christ.

We are not perfect. Ministers are not perfect, and the imperfection of those who say they are perfect, will be revealed before the Church. God will bring them down.

Sometimes there is unpleasant news about a minister, and the people think that Satan is responsible, but he is not. God brought that man down. God showed the world that his ministers are not perfect, and that they need deliverance just like everyone else. God will not tolerate pride or idolatry for any man.

He must confess that he is as vulnerable as anybody else, and that being perfect is not a qualification for preaching the gospel. One preacher said to his congregation, ***Do not idolize me because, if you idolize me, God will have to bring me down. I am not perfect.***

This woman who was clothed with the sun, had the imputed anointing of God, which cannot approach the imparted anointing of God.

The Imparted Anointing

Rom 8:29

²⁹ FOR WHOM HE DID FOREKNOW, HE ALSO DID PREDESTINATE TO BE CONFORMED TO THE IMAGE OF HIS SON, THAT HE MIGHT BE THE FIRSTBORN AMONG MANY BRETHREN. **KJV**

We are in the process of being cleansed and perfected, and will, eventually, be totally free from sin and in the image of Christ. But Jesus Christ is the only person that has completed the process. This is the imparted anointing.

Transitioning Into Christ

This woman represents the Church and those who have been called to Christ today. She has the imputed righteousness of Jesus Christ and is moving towards perfection, but she is not perfect. She has spiritual power to heal and deliver, but she is still a sinner. She is covered with the righteousness of the Lord Jesus Christ, but she still has an active sin nature.

Rev 12:2

> ² AND SHE BEING WITH CHILD **CRIED**, TRAVAILING IN BIRTH, AND PAINED TO BE DELIVERED. **KJV**

The Greek word translated *cried,* describes those who declare things publicly. Rom 9:27 says that Isaiah cried out concerning Israel. Isaiah was a preacher. The word *travail* in the Greek means *to experience the pain of childbirth, grief, and sorrow.*

Rom 9:27

> ²⁷ ESAIAS ALSO CRIETH CONCERNING ISRAEL, THOUGH THE NUMBER OF THE CHILDREN OF ISRAEL BE AS THE SAND OF THE SEA, A REMNANT SHALL BE SAVED: **KJV**

SATAN'S KINGDOM IS ENDING

Matt 24:8

⁸ ALL THESE ARE THE BEGINNING OF SORROWS. **KJV**

Mk 13:8

⁸ FOR NATION SHALL RISE AGAINST NATION, AND KINGDOM AGAINST KINGDOM: AND THERE SHALL BE EARTHQUAKES IN DIVERS PLACES, AND THERE SHALL BE FAMINES AND TROUBLES: THESE ARE THE BEGINNINGS OF SORROWS. **KJV**

The Greek word translated *sorrows* is the same word translated *cried out*. The end times are *the beginning of sorrows*.

The government of the First Adam, the rulership of the soul world of deep, raging passions and sin, is coming to an end. The world will not be destroyed, the planet will not be destroyed, the sun, moon and the universe will not be destroyed. The government that God placed in authority for His own purposes will not be destroyed. Satan, the government of the time period known as the Age of Darkness, will be destroyed. It will last only for a season, and then all of its kingdoms will come down. Satan's kingdoms are the carnal mind of mortal man.

Kingdoms are mind. We would die if we did not have a mind, so God will not take Satan's Seat down without replacing it with another kingdom. God is bringing down the pain, destruction, and torment that the carnal mind brings into our lives, and replacing it with the Kingdom of His Son, the Lord Jesus Christ. When the Kingdom of God, which is the Mind of Christ, is established as our new mind, we will stop sinning, and we will stop dying. Then, when this work has been accomplished in every human being, the pain, torment and grief that is in the earth today, will disappear.

The carnal mind
Underneath the Christ Mind

Rev 12:2

² AND SHE BEING WITH CHILD CRIED, TRAVAILING IN BIRTH, AND **PAINED** TO BE DELIVERED. **KJV**

The word *pained* is a translation of the Greek word that means *to torture, to be tested by torture, to vex, to toil, to torment, to go to the bottom.* The soul world is going to the bottom. Remember, the moon is under her feet. The soul world, our carnal mind, is going to the bottom, going underneath the Mind of Christ, but this cannot happen until the Mind of Christ has been imparted to us. We cannot be delivered from the soul world, our carnal mind, until we receive the seed of the Kingdom of God, which is the Mind of Christ.

Sometimes psychiatry helps. Sometimes casting out demons helps. But you must have the Mind of Christ to replace the kingdom of the carnal mind that is torn down.

To be pained in childbirth means that Christ Jesus is in our heart, placing the soul world, our carnal mind, under the Second Adam's feet. This means that the Kingdom of the Lord Jesus Christ must dominate the Kingdom of darkness, if we are to stop destroying ourselves. All destruction comes from within, so if it were not for Christ Jesus, we would be powerless to resist our carnal mind.

Matt 8:29

²⁹ AND, BEHOLD, THEY CRIED OUT, SAYING, WHAT HAVE WE TO DO WITH THEE, JESUS, THOU SON OF GOD? ART THOU COME HITHER TO TORMENT US BEFORE THE TIME? **KJV**

Mk 5:7

⁷ AND CRIED WITH A LOUD VOICE, AND SAID, WHAT HAVE I TO DO WITH THEE, JESUS, THOU SON OF THE MOST HIGH GOD? I ADJURE THEE BY GOD, THAT THOU TORMENT ME NOT. **KJV**

Lk 8:28

> [28] WHEN HE SAW JESUS, HE CRIED OUT, AND FELL DOWN BEFORE HIM, AND WITH A LOUD VOICE SAID, WHAT HAVE I TO DO WITH THEE, JESUS, THOU SON OF GOD MOST HIGH? I BESEECH THEE, TORMENT ME NOT. **KJV**

The word translated *cried out* also describes the torment of demons. The Scriptures talk about demons saying, *We know who you are Jesus of Nazareth, have you come to torment us before our time?*

The demons knew that they would be forced under the feet of Christ Jesus and cease to exist when the image of Jesus Christ appears. Demons (who have spiritual knowledge) knew that two thousand years would pass before the average person would began to come into the image of Jesus Christ, but they did not understand that there were two comings. They thought that Jesus come to torment them, to put the carnal mind of man under his authority and destroy them before the time.

Jesus was on the earth for only thirty-three and one-half years, so it was truly before the time that the carnal mind of the entire First Adam would be forced under the authority of Christ Jesus. Jesus cast out a few demons, but he was just one man. There will be many doing the works of God when Christ Jesus is rooted and grounded in them.

> ***Rev 12:1 – AT***: *And there appeared a great wonder in heaven, a woman, the First Adam, clothed with the imputed righteousness of God, with the moon, the soul world, the emotions of her carnal mind in total submission to Christ Jesus, who is symbolized by a crown that covers her head, the authority of twelve stars of the government of God. (ATB)*

Pregnant with the Christ Child

The Church is the government of God in the earth today. In the Old Testament, the government of God was vested in national Israel.

Rev 12:2

² AND SHE BEING WITH CHILD . . . . **KJV**

This spiritual woman typifies the whole soul that is pregnant with the Christ child. The Holy Spirit enters into the heart of the individual members of that soul and begins to form the Christ child, the image of God, in each and every one. We are saved by the life of Christ when he is fully born and dwells in us permanently. He is our righteousness, our faith, and our life. We no longer live by the life of the fallen First Adam, which causes us to die. We live by the life of the indwelling Christ child.

The spiritual woman who was with child *cried out*, meaning, she was preaching. *Preaching* does not necessarily mean from a pulpit. The internalized Christ can send you, sometimes to a total stranger, to deliver his message for that person. *Being sent* is a sign that you may be pregnant with the Christ child.

The Purpose of Trials

Rev 12:2

² . . . TRAVAILING IN BIRTH. . . . **KJV**

Did you ever wonder why there are trials in our lives? Did you ever think, *Why is God doing this to me?* Then, because you did not understand, you tried in every way you could think of to get out of the trial. But Peter said that we should not be surprised when fiery trials come are way.

Christ Jesus can fully rule and reign over the carnal mind only after it is broken it up and its parts are rearranged in the proper order. So, Christ Jesus afflicts the First Adam with fiery trials to bring the emotions and the thoughts of the carnal mind under his authority.

No one likes to go through trials, but that is the way the Lord set up, and He is smarter than we are. If we could only understand that God is for us and not against us, and that the emergence of Christ Jesus, the government of God, is the result of the trials, they would be more tolerable.

Rev 12:2

> [2] ... AND PAINED TO BE DELIVERED. **KJV**

The word ***delivered*** means to ***bear fruit***. Christians are expected to bear fruit.

Deut 7:13

> [13] AND HE WILL LOVE THEE, AND BLESS THEE, AND MULTIPLY THEE: HE WILL ALSO BLESS THE FRUIT OF THY WOMB, AND THE FRUIT OF THY LAND, THY CORN, AND THY WINE, AND THINE OIL, THE INCREASE OF THY KINE, AND THE FLOCKS OF THY SHEEP, IN THE LAND WHICH HE SWARE UNTO THY FATHERS TO GIVE THEE. **KJV**

Prov 12:12

> [12] THE WICKED DESIRETH THE NET OF EVIL MEN: BUT THE ROOT OF THE RIGHTEOUS YIELDETH FRUIT. **KJV**

Children are the fruit of a woman's womb, and the Christ child is the spiritual fruit of righteousness.

Matt 13:8

> [8] BUT OTHER FELL INTO GOOD GROUND, AND BROUGHT FORTH FRUIT, SOME AN HUNDREDFOLD, SOME SIXTYFOLD, SOME THIRTYFOLD. **KJV**

Heb 12:11

> [11] NOW NO CHASTENING FOR THE PRESENT SEEMETH TO BE JOYOUS, BUT GRIEVOUS: NEVERTHELESS AFTERWARD IT YIELDETH THE PEACEABLE FRUIT OF RIGHTEOUSNESS UNTO THEM WHICH ARE EXERCISED THEREBY. **KJV**

1 Jn 2:29

> ²⁹ IF YE KNOW THAT HE IS RIGHTEOUS, YE KNOW THAT EVERY ONE THAT DOETH RIGHTEOUSNESS IS BORN OF HIM. **KJV**

2 Cor 5:21

> ²¹ FOR HE HATH MADE HIM TO BE SIN FOR US, WHO KNEW NO SIN; THAT WE MIGHT BE MADE THE RIGHTEOUSNESS OF GOD IN HIM. **KJV**

Everyone that doeth righteousness is born of God. Chastening produces the fruit of righteousness, and trials witness to the birthing.

The Dragon

Rev 12:3

> ³ AND THERE APPEARED ANOTHER WONDER IN HEAVEN; AND BEHOLD A GREAT RED DRAGON, HAVING SEVEN HEADS AND TEN HORNS, AND SEVEN CROWNS UPON HIS HEADS. **KJV**

This Dragon speaks of authority and spiritual power. The Greek word translated **red, flame-like color** or **having the color of fire,** Strong's #4450, also means the actual *fire*.

This Greek word, which indicates **spiritual power** in the Scripture, is from a root word that is translated **lightning**. In the Old Testament, **red** and **Adam** are translated from the same Hebrew word that is translated *fire*. These are strong witnesses that the Dragon is the nature of the fallen creation (the First Adam). One more time, **the Dragon is the nature of the fallen creation**, a flaming Serpent with spiritual power.

Isaiah prophesies about the Seraphim, the flaming serpents with six wings that surround the throne of God. ***Six*** is the number of man, and **wings** indicate that God has elevated man into the heavenlies where he is exalting, glorifying, and surrounding God as a part of the glorified creation.

This is a witness that *fallen man* (the First Adam) has the Serpent's nature, and is actually *the express image of the Serpent*. This is a hard word. 2nd Thessalonians says that Christ Jesus will appear when the man of sin is revealed. If we could only receive the truth that the fallen First Adam has the nature of the Serpent, God would deliver us and reform us into His likeness (nature). Then we would understand why we will continue to be the enemies of God until our spirit is redeemed and our soul is adopted. But we have to recognize our fallen spiritual condition before the Son of God will appear in us.

He is great and has authority. He is red, he has spiritual power, and is a Dragon, a fascinating Dragon. The word for **Dragon** is ***Strong's*** #1404, the word that indicates *witchcraft*. He had seven heads and ten horns.

Rev 17:7

> ⁷ AND THE ANGEL SAID UNTO ME, WHEREFORE DIDST THOU MARVEL? I WILL TELL THEE THE MYSTERY OF THE WOMAN, AND OF THE BEAST THAT CARRIETH HER, WHICH HATH THE SEVEN HEADS AND TEN HORNS. **KJV**

The beast has seven heads and ten horns. *Seven* is the number of fulfillment, and *heads* indicates the number of powers that the beast possesses. *Seven heads* indicates that the beast's powers are complete.

God told the righteous First Adam to reproduce, but it is the fallen First Adam who has multiplied unto his fullness (as indicated by the number seven).

He also has ten horns. *Horns* mean *power*. The number *ten* signifies *the Law*. The dead soul is the world of the Law, the place where the Law has power, and the Law has power wherever sin reigns.

We all exist in the world of the Law, the world of the First Adam. The Law is for people who cannot distinguish between right and what is wrong. It would be irrational to tell an honest person to stop stealing. We sin because we do not know how to live in obedience to the Law of God. We need a Law, and we need to be taught how to obey that Law.

Out of Order

Fallen Adam has multiplied to his fullness, and has spiritual authority in the world of the Law. There are seven crowns upon his seven heads. Rev 17 says that the beast has seven heads and ten horns, and is filled with the names of blasphemy. In Rev 12, the Dragon has seven heads, ten horns and seven crowns. This Dragon has spiritual authority over God's people, and is ruling. He is not underfoot, he is ruling. He is in the wrong moral order in relation to Christ Jesus.

The spirit (mind) is in proper order, and the soul (personality) is in proper order, but the darkness called Satan, who exists to give form to the creation, is not in proper order. He is not underfoot where he is supposed to be, but he is, nevertheless, ruling. He has great power, and goes after the woman to devour her child.

A False Anointing

Rev 17:3

> ³ . . . AND I SAW A WOMAN SIT UPON A SCARLET COLOURED BEAST, FULL OF NAMES OF BLASPHEMY, HAVING SEVEN HEADS AND TEN HORNS. **KJV**

The color of the beast is *scarlet*, as opposed to the Dragon, which is *red*. The word *red* means *fire*, spiritual power, but the word *scarlet* means *to be dyed red*. It is a false anointing. It is not the true spiritual power of God. It is a reflection of the Dragon's spiritual power. The beast has borrowed from the color (spiritual power) of the Dragon. He does not have his own spiritual power.

He has seven heads and ten horns, has multiplied to the fullest extent possible in the world of the Law, and is filled with the names of blasphemy. All the wickedness born from Satan's adulterous relationship with the spirit of the carnal mind is present. He has reached spiritual maturity and is filling many evil-speaking, spiritual children with his unholy thoughts.

The fallen First Adam is Satan's victim. This is the condition of the First Adam. God is supposed to be ruling over the Righteous First Adam, but Satan is ruling in His place. The spiritual power that was created to give form to the First Adam, rose up and replaced the power of God. This is the spirit of antichrist. So, the fallen First Adam died and Satan, that adulterous power, is now ruling over Him. Satan came up out of his place under the First Adam's authority, and is now ruling over Him.

There are three parts to the living soul. One part rose up and is ruling the other two parts, and their illegal relationship has produced all of the names of blasphemy. Today, God is putting Satan back down under the First Adam's feet, but Satan does not want to go. He is fighting like the wild, venomous beast that he is.

Deception and Seduction

Rev 12:4

> 4 AND HIS TAIL DREW THE THIRD PART OF THE STARS OF HEAVEN, AND DID CAST THEM TO THE EARTH: . . . . **KJV**

We have already established that the stars of heaven are the government of God, and that, in Daniel 8, truth was cast to the ground. He deceived one-third of the government of God that exists in the Church today. He stole God's revelation from the Church, and cast the preachers, who are carnal men preaching carnality from a position of authority, to the ground. Most of the preachers today are not spiritual men, and the people are being hurt, but God will deliver them.

Rev 12:4

⁴ . . . AND THE DRAGON STOOD BEFORE THE WOMAN WHICH WAS READY TO BE DELIVERED, FOR TO DEVOUR HER CHILD AS SOON AS IT WAS BORN. **KJV**

The Dragon is within the collective group of believers who are bringing forth the Christ child.

Dan 8:11-12

¹¹ YEA, HE MAGNIFIED HIMSELF EVEN TO THE PRINCE OF THE HOST, AND BY HIM THE DAILY SACRIFICE WAS TAKEN AWAY, AND THE PLACE OF HIS SANCTUARY WAS CAST DOWN.

¹² AND AN HOST WAS GIVEN HIM AGAINST THE DAILY SACRIFICE BY REASON OF TRANSGRESSION, AND IT CAST DOWN THE TRUTH TO THE GROUND; AND IT PRACTISED, AND PROSPERED. **KJV**

There is a lie in the government of God today. One-third of the Church world is preaching lies, and that lie is prospering. *It practiced and it prospered*. The Greek word translated *practiced* means *to produce or create, to produce by labor, to make fruit, to make or prepare an offering, to wage war with*. It also is an idiom for *sexual intercourse*.

The Serpent usurped God's authority, and is now fornicating with the spirit of the First Adam. He has replaced God, married God's bride, and is fornicating with her. The Serpent rose up and seduced the spirit of the First Adam and he died.

He drew one-third of the stars with his tail. The Greek word *tail* means *back end, unseen, hidden, dark side, unconscious mind*. Satan rose up from the unconscious part of the mind of one-third of the ministers of God, and deceived them.[1]

Satan seduced them from deep in the unconscious part of their mind. These ministers are defenseless against this kind of

---

[1] Sheila R. Vitale, *The Seduction Of Eve* (Long Island: Living Epistles Ministries, 2016). Available on Amazon.com

attack, because they reject deliverance. They reject the reality that the darkness is within all of us. They are not looking for deception within themselves. They think that they are perfect from the day that they receive Christ, so they are being seduced despite the protection afforded to us by the blood of Jesus. They look for seduction only in other people, so they are overtaken by the spiritual witch in the unconscious part of their own mind.

Because of this misunderstanding, many preachers have become, for all intents and purposes, carnal men in the image of Satan, preaching Satan's doctrine from their pulpits. They are in the pulpit moving in the gifts, because the gifts and the calling of God are without repentance. They can be healing and prophesying by the Spirit of God and, while their doctrinal revelation is in the image of Satan. This is the mystery of how a minister of God can bring forth Satan's doctrine.

Rev 12:4

> [4] . . . THE DRAGON STOOD BEFORE THE WOMAN WHICH WAS READY TO BE DELIVERED, FOR TO DEVOUR HER CHILD AS SOON AS IT WAS BORN. **KJV**

The Dragon is the emotions of the woman who is in the world of souls. He is supposed to be under the authority of Christ, but he is not. He is confronting the Woman face-to-face, manipulating her emotions either as fear or disbelief, and is ready to devour the Christ child that God is bringing forth within her.

Gal 5:15

> [15] BUT IF YE BITE AND DEVOUR ONE ANOTHER, TAKE HEED THAT YE BE NOT CONSUMED ONE OF ANOTHER. **KJV**

Ps 14:4

> [4] . . . ALL THE WORKERS OF INIQUITY NO KNOWLEDGE? WHO EAT UP MY PEOPLE AS THEY EAT BREAD . . . . **KJV**

Satan, the agent of the Serpent within the evil children that he has produced through the spirit of the individual mind, would devour the human soul, as well as the Christ child, if he could.

One Spiritual Creation

This woman with her emotions, the moon under her feet, is the First Adam. The Dragon is a part of the First Adam, one of all the parts that form the creation.

Gen 3:6

> ⁶ ... SHE TOOK OF THE FRUIT THEREOF, AND DID EAT, AND GAVE ALSO UNTO HER HUSBAND WITH HER; AND HE DID EAT. **KJV**

The righteous mind of the woman was present with her. They were one. Even though the Lord breaks the parts of the First Adam down for us so that we can understand it, the female (spirit of the mind), the crown (Jehovah's righteous mind), the Dragon (the nature of the earth), and the Christ child (God's righteous nature being born in the individual), are all one spiritual entity that is appearing as a woman in Revelation, Chapter 12.

Rev 12:1-4

> ¹ AND THERE APPEARED A GREAT WONDER IN HEAVEN; A WOMAN CLOTHED WITH THE SUN, AND THE MOON UNDER HER FEET, AND UPON HER HEAD A CROWN OF TWELVE STARS:
>
> ² AND SHE BEING WITH CHILD CRIED, TRAVAILING IN BIRTH, AND PAINED TO BE DELIVERED.
>
> ³ AND THERE APPEARED ANOTHER WONDER IN HEAVEN; AND BEHOLD A GREAT RED DRAGON, HAVING SEVEN HEADS AND TEN HORNS, AND SEVEN CROWNS UPON HIS HEADS.
>
> ⁴ AND HIS TAIL DREW THE THIRD PART OF THE STARS OF HEAVEN, AND DID CAST THEM TO THE EARTH: AND THE DRAGON STOOD BEFORE THE WOMAN WHICH WAS READY TO

BE DELIVERED, FOR TO DEVOUR HER CHILD AS SOON AS IT WAS BORN. **KJV**

All of the symbols in these Scriptures are aspects of the First Adam, and the whole panorama that we see in Rev 12:1-4 is taking place within the mind of the believer.

Everything is happening on the spiritual plane within us. The woman, the moon, the crown, the Serpent, his tail, and the child that is ready to be born are all within us.

The Son Abides Forever

Jn 8:35

³⁵ AND THE SERVANT ABIDETH NOT IN THE HOUSE FOR EVER: BUT THE SON ABIDETH EVER. **KJV**

The servant does not abide in the house forever. The fallen First Adam who has received the gifts and calling of God, is the servant who does not abide in the house forever. Christ, the Son, when he is birthed in us, will abide forever. When the Christ child, the Son of God, is birthed in us, He will never leave us, and we will live forever.

The natural world is the mirror image of the spiritual world. The events of the spiritual world appear very different in the material world. When a woman has a baby in the natural world, that baby leaves her body, grows up, and leads an independent life. In the spiritual world, the Christ child does not leave our body when it is born, but becomes our new, spiritual mind. He abides forever, and, according to Jn 8, we live by His life.

1 Tim 2:15

¹⁵ . . . SHE SHALL BE SAVED IN CHILDBEARING . . . .
KJV

The fallen spirit of our carnal mind is the female aspect of the First Adam. When she births the Christ child, He does not leave our body, He joins Himself to us, and we become one. That is how we are saved by His life.

Rom 5:10

> ¹⁰ FOR IF, WHEN WE WERE ENEMIES, WE WERE RECONCILED TO GOD BY THE DEATH OF HIS SON, MUCH MORE, BEING RECONCILED, WE SHALL BE SAVED BY HIS LIFE. **KJV**

We are saved by the life of Christ because His life does not leave us. It joins itself to us and becomes one with us.

The child that the woman is pregnant with is Christ.

Rev 12:5

> ⁵ . . . MAN CHILD, WHO WAS TO RULE ALL NATIONS WITH A ROD OF IRON: . . . . **KJV**

Rev 1:5

> ⁵ AND FROM JESUS CHRIST, WHO IS THE FAITHFUL WITNESS, AND THE FIRST BEGOTTEN OF THE DEAD, ... **KJV**

Soul Man to Spiritual Man

The soul world is the world of death. The Scriptural definition of death is the carnal mind. Paul says that if we think with the thoughts of the natural man, we are dead. This is a radical definition of death for people who do not read the Bible, because we are walking around, talking, marrying, and producing children. Jesus of Nazareth is the first cell of the First Adam to be restored to the life of God. This means that the thoughts of Jesus' carnal mind were completely nullified

Jesus was the first man to be raised up out of the world of death. The Christ within Jesus of Nazareth joined Himself to the soul of the natural man, Jesus, they became one man. and Jesus ascended into the heavenlies by the power of the Shekinah that

Christ was attached to. Jesus is doing the same for us today. This is the ultimate end of Jesus' purpose for us: To become one with us, until we ascend by his Spirit into the heavenlies where He is. But our bodies will not ascend with us.

We are not flying away in a rapture. Our spiritual condition is being elevated from soul man to spiritual man. Christ is joining Himself to us and taking us up to where Jesus is. There is no way to ascend from the soul world to the spiritual world other than by Christ joining Himself to us, and taking us with Him.

We will receive spiritual bodies at a future time, after a season of experiencing the power of an ascended mind (the condition that Jesus was in the days of His flesh).

Germany and Japan were devastated from WWII. There was no food in those countries and many homes were destroyed, so many German and Japanese women wanted to go to America. Marriage to an American serviceman was the only way a German or a Japanese woman could become an American citizen. so many of them married American soldiers. ***It is a great mystery, but a married couple is one flesh***.

Many European and Japanese women received permission to come to the United States with their American husbands because the world recognizes that when a woman marries a man, the two become one soul, and when he goes home to the United States of America, even though you are Japanese or German, you have the right to live in America with him, and you also have the right to American Citizenship. This is what is happening to us in the Spirit. There is no way we can get into the spiritual world of God on our own. But we are now citizens of Heaven because Jesus Christ is marrying us.

It is a great mystery that we are becoming one with Christ Jesus and shall go home with Him to His Father. We are kings and priests because His Holy child dwells in us.

Rev 1:5

Satan Swallowed Up/ Satan's Kingdom Is Ending

> ⁵ AND FROM JESUS CHRIST, WHO IS THE FAITHFUL WITNESS, AND THE FIRST BEGOTTEN OF THE DEAD, AND THE PRINCE OF THE KINGS OF THE EARTH. UNTO HIM THAT LOVED US, AND WASHED US FROM OUR SINS IN HIS OWN BLOOD, ... **KJV**

Bringing Forth the Holy Child

Jesus is the Prince of the kings of the earth, and we are the kings of the earth, because the Holy child dwells in us.

> **Acts 4:27-30**
>
> ²⁷ FOR OF A TRUTH AGAINST THY HOLY CHILD JESUS, WHOM THOU HAST ANOINTED, BOTH HEROD, AND PONTIUS PILATE, WITH THE GENTILES, AND THE PEOPLE OF ISRAEL, WERE GATHERED TOGETHER,
>
> ²⁸ FOR TO DO WHATSOEVER THY HAND AND THY COUNSEL DETERMINED BEFORE TO BE DONE.
>
> ²⁹ AND NOW, LORD, BEHOLD THEIR THREATENINGS: AND GRANT UNTO THY SERVANTS, THAT WITH ALL BOLDNESS THEY MAY SPEAK THY WORD,
>
> ³⁰ BY STRETCHING FORTH THINE HAND TO HEAL; AND THAT SIGNS AND WONDERS MAY BE DONE BY THE NAME OF THY HOLY CHILD JESUS. **KJV**

Pontius Pilot and Herod threatened to do damage to the Holy child Jesus within the apostles. Jesus was already crucified and resurrected at this time, so we know that the Scripture is not talking about Jesus' physical body, but about Peter and John who are saying, *Raise up your hand, stretch forth your hand and do mighty signs and wonders through us in the name of thy Holy child*.

Jesus had already been crucified, so the apostles were asking that the Christ child within them do the works of Jesus.

Names represent spirit, so they were saying in their prayer to the Father, *Impart to us the ability to do the same works that*

Jesus did; that the Holy child, this spiritual entity that was in the man known as Jesus of Nazareth, should also be in Peter and John, the two servants of God that were praying this prayer.

Peter and John were saying, **Let the Spirit that was in Jesus of Nazareth be in us.** Christ and the Father were in Jesus of Nazareth, who is now one with the Father; and the glorified Jesus Christ is now in us by His Spirit, and bringing forth His Holy child in us.

Ruling by the Indwelling Christ

Rev 19:15

> [15] ...HE SHOULD SMITE THE NATIONS: AND HE SHALL RULE THEM WITH A ROD OF IRON: .... **KJV**

The nations are in our flesh. They are the demonic powers and elements of the soul that are in our flesh. He will rule over them. This is the Christ child that is coming forth in us, He will rule them with a rod of iron.

Rods in the Scripture refer to *the tongue*. He will rule by the spoken word. *Iron* signifies *great power*. He is going to rule by a powerful spoken word, and legitimate power only comes from the Spirit of God. He will rule from the Spirit of God that is in this Christ child, who is deep within our hearts. Our souls and our bodies must come into submission to the indwelling Christ.

Rev. 2:27

> [27] AND HE SHALL RULE THEM WITH A ROD OF IRON; AS THE VESSELS OF A POTTER SHALL THEY BE BROKEN TO SHIVERS: ... **KJV**

Our soul and body are made of clay. The glorified Jesus Christ, by the Christ child within us, is breaking the First Adam's fallen soul within us to shivers, and putting it back together again in the proper moral order which will restore eternal life to us.

Jesus is the one speaking in Revelation, Chapter 1, the one who overcame. Jesus is the overcomer of the book of Revelation.

Jn 16:33

^{33} . . . BE OF GOOD CHEER; I HAVE OVERCOME THE WORLD. **KJV**

Jesus Christ is the overcomer, and now we, too, have the opportunity, in Him, to overcome also. We can do nothing of ourselves.

There is a big move in the Church today to say, ***You do it, stand up, try harder***. But the truth is that we can do nothing of ourselves. We overcome only by the Christ within us, who empowers us. We cannot sit back and do nothing. When all of our efforts come from the indwelling Christ, there can be no failure because it is Him in us doing the work.

CHRIST OVERCOMING IN US

The Law of Moses

Col 2:13-14

¹³ AND YOU, BEING DEAD IN YOUR SINS AND THE UNCIRCUMCISION OF YOUR FLESH, HATH HE QUICKENED TOGETHER WITH HIM, HAVING FORGIVEN YOU ALL TRESPASSES;

¹⁴ BLOTTING OUT THE HANDWRITING OF ORDINANCES THAT WAS AGAINST US, WHICH WAS CONTRARY TO US, AND TOOK IT OUT OF THE WAY, NAILING IT TO HIS CROSS; **KJV**

This Scripture is a victorious Scripture, but it has been preached without understanding.

The Law is Spiritual

The Greek word translated ***blot out*** sounds like a negative word, but on the contrary, it means ***to make complete*** and ***to wash or anoint in every part***. The handwriting of ordinances is the Law of Moses. The Law of God is spiritual, but man cannot understand spiritual things. So God instructed Moses to write a book of ordinances, statutes, and commandments, to help man at least repent when he does sin. It is impossible for the fallen First Adam to keep the spiritual Law of God in his own power.

The handwriting of ordinances that is against us is the Law of Moses. It is contrary to us because the natural man, by his fallen nature, sins continually, and the Law of God stands up to convict him of his sins. If we do not know that hating our brother (as a spiritual example) is wrong, if we do not know that fornication is wrong, we would be fornicating, and very happy about it. But the Law of God stands up in front of us and says, ***Thou shalt not fornicate.*** That is how the Law is against us.

It is our fallen nature to want to fornicate. Human sexuality is not a sin as many people believe it to be. It is a natural human instinct, but it is only legal according to God's Law in marriage. If the Lord God did not stand up and say, ***Human sexuality is not fornication in marriage, but you are not to copulate outside of marriage***, we would not know that fornication is wrong, and our natural instincts would drive us to fornicate on a regular basis. The Law of God opposes the natural instincts of the fallen First Adam.

The Law is Contrary to Human Nature

The Law is against our very human nature, and directly opposes it. If we did not know that it was wrong to take another's coat, if we did not have the Law, when we saw something that we liked, we would pick it up and walk away with it. But the Law of God says, ***Thou shalt not steal.*** The nature that man is born with is in direct opposition to the spiritual Law of God, so there is a conflict every time that we are confronted with the temptation to sin.

Col 2:13

[13] AND YOU, BEING DEAD IN YOUR SINS AND THE UNCIRCUMCISION OF YOUR FLESH, HATH HE QUICKENED TOGETHER WITH HIM, HAVING FORGIVEN YOU ALL TRESPASSES; **KJV**

The Law of Moses opposes every fallen thought, but Jesus took them out of the way, and nailed them to His cross.

Rom 3:20

[20] ... BY THE LAW IS THE KNOWLEDGE OF SIN. **KJV**

That is the function of the Law, to convict us of sin. It was never intended to bring us to salvation.

Christ Jesus, the Fulfillment of the Law

Matt 5:17

¹⁷ . . . I AM NOT COME TO DESTROY, BUT TO FULFIL. **KJV**

Rom 10:4

⁴ FOR CHRIST IS THE END OF THE LAW FOR RIGHTEOUSNESS TO EVERY ONE THAT BELIEVETH. **KJV**

What is the fulfillment of the Law? The fulfillment of the Law is the ability to keep the Law. Fallen man cannot keep the Law in his own strength, and national Israel could not keep the Law, either. God permitted them to sacrifice animals (a type of offering up their own sinful flesh), so that they should not be destroyed because of their sins.

God said, *I am giving you these Laws and ordinances, and will let you sacrifice animals for a season, but I am going to make a New Covenant with you. The day is coming that I will impart the power to you to keep my spiritual Law. You will not have to sacrifice animals, symbolizing your own death anymore, because death is the result of sin.* Death is the penalty for sin.

. . . I will cover you, I will protect you. You can be saved through obedience to the Law. If you sacrifice an animal, I will not take your life, but this provision is only temporary until I impart the power to you to keep my spiritual Law.

Our ability to keep the spiritual Law of God (a process that takes years) is in Christ Jesus. We receive that power when He dwells in us.

The words *blotting out*, mean *to make complete*, and *to wash in every part*. Jesus Christ came to fulfill the spiritual Law of God, not the written Law of Moses which represented the spiritual Law of God that fallen Adam was unable to keep. Jesus does this by filling up, with His own righteous Mind, every hole in our fallen nature that makes us break the Law. He joins Himself to us and gives us whatever we are lacking that causes us to break the spiritual Law of God. This spiritual experience that washes and anoints us is available through Jesus' glorified life.

Lk 23:31

> ³¹ FOR IF THEY DO THESE THINGS IN A GREEN TREE, WHAT SHALL BE DONE IN THE DRY? **KJV**

A man that Jesus was ministering to said, *I see them walking as trees.* The natural man kills the Son of God! If that is what he does to a man that is filled with the life of God, what will he do to the dry trees? What will they do to fallen men that Christ is growing up in, who have not been completed yet?

Eph 2:15

> ¹⁵ HAVING ABOLISHED IN HIS FLESH THE ENMITY, EVEN THE LAW OF COMMANDMENTS CONTAINED IN ORDINANCES; FOR TO MAKE IN HIMSELF OF TWAIN ONE NEW MAN, SO MAKING PEACE; **KJV**

The Law of Ordinances subjects us to the Sowing & Reaping Judgment, which is enforced by the Satanic world in the midst of us. Satan rules over us until Christ is grafted to us and brings us to holiness. Jesus took the Law out from the midst of us and replaced it with Himself, even Christ, our hope of glorification. That is how Jesus fulfilled the Law.

Jesus blotted out the handwriting of the ordinances that were against us by filling in the empty space in our soul. Christ Jesus is the spiritual brains of fallen man. He is the knowledge, understanding, and power of God that equips us to keep the spiritual Law of God. The Law of Ordinances was contrary to us, but Jesus took it out of the way by equipping us to keep the spiritual Law of God.

Jesus nailed the Law of Ordinances to His cross. Who is Jesus' cross? Jesus' cross in this context was not a piece of wood that the Romans nailed him to. We are talking about spiritual things here. A cross comes from a piece of wood, and as indicated above, unsaved men are made of spiritual dry wood. So, spiritually speaking we are trees.

Jesus referred to Himself as a green tree. Whoever does not have the Spirit of God is a dry tree. Jesus Christ nailed himself to us in the form of Christ Jesus. Jesus nailed Himself to the First Adam, and made us one. We are His cross. But, being joined to us did not contaminate or kill Him. On the contrary, we have been saved and washed clean.

<u>Col 2:15</u>

> ¹⁵ AND HAVING SPOILED PRINCIPALITIES AND POWERS, HE MADE A SHEW OF THEM OPENLY, TRIUMPHING OVER THEM IN IT. **KJV**

The Greek word translated ***spoiled*** means that ***Christ destroyed them***. He nailed Himself to a cross. The word ***nailed*** means something that fastens one thing to something else. The Scripture says, ***triumphing over them in it***. The word *it* is a reflexive pronoun, and it really means ***Himself***. This work that Christ Jesus did, He did it within the man known as Jesus of Nazareth.

Jesus was a natural man who was tempted by Satan. He was with the beasts of the field (Mk 1:13). This means that Jesus' carnal mind was cleansed with the washing of water by the Word. He was polarized, that is, the carnal mind and the Christ Mind in Jesus were completely separated, and His Christ Mind dominated His carnal mind.

What do the words ***open show*** mean? What did Jesus do? He spoiled principalities and powers and made an open show of them, triumphing over them in Himself. Christ Jesus was the Son of God incarnated in Jesus, a natural man. Christ Jesus lived in a vessel with the beasts of the field, the carnal mind that Jesus received from His parents, and Christ Jesus triumphed over that carnal mind that was a part of the natural man, Jesus, His other self.

Triumphing over them in Himself. Christ Jesus within the man, Jesus, swallowed them up Satan, the Dragon, and the woman. They all lost their individual identities, and became one soul that Christ Jesus was nailed to.

<u>**Matt 28:20**</u>

[20] . . . AND, LO, I AM WITH YOU ALWAY, EVEN UNTO THE END OF THE WORLD. **KJV**

Christ Jesus will never leave us. He will live within mankind for the life of the ages, and, because He lives in us, we have His righteousness.

<u>**Eph 2:13-15**</u>

[13] BUT NOW IN CHRIST JESUS YE WHO SOMETIMES WERE FAR OFF ARE MADE NIGH BY THE BLOOD OF CHRIST.

[14] FOR HE IS OUR PEACE, WHO HATH MADE BOTH ONE, AND HATH BROKEN DOWN THE MIDDLE WALL OF PARTITION BETWEEN US;

[15] HAVING ABOLISHED IN HIS FLESH THE ENMITY, EVEN THE LAW OF COMMANDMENTS CONTAINED IN ORDINANCES; FOR TO MAKE IN HIMSELF OF TWAIN ONE NEW MAN, SO MAKING PEACE; **KJV**

The middle wall that Jesus knocked down separates us from Him. Both Christ and fallen Adam are within us, and there is a wall between the two. Christ Jesus within the man Jesus, knocked down that wall, and made one Christ Mind of Jesus' carnal mind and Jesus' Christ Mind. That is how Christ Jesus abolished the enmity in Jesus' flesh.

Satan is the enmity in our flesh, who tempts us to sin and then punishes us with the Sowing & Reaping Judgment when we do sin. Satan is the unconscious part of our carnal mind. That is how Satan was able to tempt Jesus. He was tempted by His own carnal mind. Christ Jesus, the Spiritual Law of God, has abolished the carnal mind of the natural man, which is subject to the Law of Ordinances, the Law that condemns the natural man.

Rom 7:20-23

[20] NOW IF I DO THAT I WOULD NOT, IT IS NO MORE I THAT DO IT, BUT SIN THAT DWELLETH IN ME.

[21] I FIND THEN A LAW, THAT, WHEN I WOULD DO GOOD, EVIL IS PRESENT WITH ME.

[22] FOR I DELIGHT IN THE LAW OF GOD AFTER THE INWARD MAN:

[23] BUT I SEE ANOTHER LAW IN MY MEMBERS, WARRING AGAINST THE LAW OF MY MIND, AND BRINGING ME INTO CAPTIVITY TO THE LAW OF SIN WHICH IS IN MY MEMBERS.
KJV

The Law of sin is the world of the soul that Christ Jesus nailed Himself to. *. . . that he might reconcile both unto God* [both Christ and fallen Adam] *in one body [in this body, in your body, in my body] by the cross* [spiritual power that was released when the two were joined], *having slain the enmity thereby.*

Where is your cross? Where is your torture stake, where is your piece of wood? It is your First Adam. Today Christ Jesus is in the process of nailing Himself to us, and when that process is complete, we will be completely reconciled to God. Our carnal mind, fallen Adam, will have been swallowed up, and our personality will no longer be fallen, or unclean, but will be dwelling in heavenly places with Christ Jesus.

If you have been incarnated at the express will of the Father, these are the signs that follow you. You have the imputed anointing. Now, Christ is not necessarily manifesting at this moment in everyone who has the seed, but if you have been incarnated at the will of the Father, this will happen to you at some time in your life. You will manifest the imputed anointing, you will birth the Christ child, and you will experience separation, or sanctification, which is the polarizing of the two minds of fallen Adam and Christ within you.

The thoughts of Christ must be separated from the thoughts of fallen Adam. It is a painful process. We call it tribulation. Satan will be chained in the bottomless pit, which we read about in the book of Revelation. The thoughts of Christ will be separated from the thoughts of fallen Adam, Christ will rise up and rule over the whole First Adam and Satan will be underfoot, chained to the bottom of the pit that Adam, the living soul, fell into when He died. Satan will be swallowed up, and, ultimately, the promise is that we will be glorified, which is deliverance from our solid physical body.

We will be given a glorified body that will not get sick, grow old, or die. It already happened to Jesus, the only man born of a woman that this happened to, but the promise is for everybody.

Three Trimesters

Matt 13:8

> ⁸ BUT OTHER FELL INTO GOOD GROUND, AND BROUGHT FORTH FRUIT, SOME AN HUNDREDFOLD, SOME SIXTYFOLD, SOME THIRTYFOLD. **KJV**

The Christ child is birthed in three trimesters. Jesus referred to it as the 30-fold, the 60-fold, and 100-fold. The 30-fold birthing of the Christ is typified by faith. If you hear the Gospel preached and believe, you have birthed a 30-fold manifestation of the Christ child, because you cannot believe if He has not empowered you to believe.

The 60-fold is typified by power. When the Holy Ghost comes upon you, you shall have power. The sign that you are moving in the 60-fold world is that you have the power to heal and cast out evil spirits.

The sign that you have birthed the Christ, the 100-fold, which is the fullness, is that you will stop dying. Jesus Christ is the only one born of a woman that manifested the fullness of God without measure, but it is a promise for all of us as we grow and mature in Him.

But, we should not say to one another, *You are 30-fold, I am 60-fold, you are a tare, I am a wheat.* Such thoughts are spiritual childishness. People who say things like that do not understand the Scripture. The promise is for everyone.

Christ Triumphant

Some preach that there will be wood choppers and water bearers in the kingdom. No, we will all get to the same place but at different times. We only have to finish the race. It does not matter how fast we run, only that we finish. The ultimate end is that God will be all in all, fully manifested in every human being on the earth.

When we all have the Mind of Christ, there will be no need for leadership, no need for preachers, no need for a government in Washington, or in any country that could be corrupt. Everybody will have the perfect Mind of Christ, and we will all be in agreement. Christ Jesus will be ruling in every individual.

There will be no more wars or bickering, not on the governmental level, in marriages, or between mothers and children, because we will all have the righteous thoughts of God. Selfishness is the cause of bickering among people. Everyone is looking out for his own interest, which is carnal thinking.

The Mind of Christ thinks for the good of the many. We will all be in agreement. There will be no conflict. Peace will rule and reign in this earth, the lion will truly lie down with the lamb, and all of the promises, the wonderful promises of peace in the earth and good will towards men, shall be accomplished.

Christ within the man Jesus nailed Himself to the cross, which is fallen Adam, the First Adam, thus making one new man within Himself, who was able to triumph over Satan and the other powers and principalities that rule in the carnal mind. Christ Jesus

Satan Swallowed Up/ Christ Overcoming In Us

made an open show of them by utterly stripping them of their powers to keep him in the grave. Today Christ is in the earth doing the same thing in every one of us.

PROPHECY

    Yea, saith the Lord, I shall fill thee, saith God, yea I shall surely fill the empty places, saith God, and I shall make the valleys flat, saith the Lord, I shall bring down the high mountains, saith God, and I shall make all even in my peace, saith the Lord, and I shall deliver thee and thy need for these things, saith God. Yea, I shall give thee thy security, I shall indeed be thy security, saith God, and I shall deliver thee from thy fear, and thou shalt be tormented no longer, saith the Lord.

TABLE OF REFERENCES

1

1 Cor 11:3 10
1 Jn 2:29 18
1 Tim 2:15 25

2

2 Cor 5:21 18

A

Acts 4:27-30 28

C

Col 2:13 32
Col 2:13-14 31
Col 2:15 35

D

Dan 8:11 .... 8, 9
Dan 8:11-12 22
Dan 8:12 9
Deut 7:13 17

E

Eph 2:13-15 36
Eph 2:15 34

G

Gal 2:20 9
Gal 5:15 23
Gen 3:6 24
Gen 37:9-10 4

H

Heb 12:11 17
Heb 2:6-8 5

J

Jer 31:27 2
Jn 16:33 30
Jn 8:35 25

L

Lk 23:31 34
Lk 8:28 15

M

Mal 4:2 4
Matt 13:8 .... 17, 38
Matt 24:8 13
Matt 28:20 36
Matt 5:17 33
Matt 8:29 14
Mk 13:8 13
Mk 5:7 14

P

Prov 12:12 17
Ps 136:9 7
Ps 14:4 23
Ps 84:11 3

R

Rev 1:20 7

Satan Swallowed Up/ Table Of References

Rev 1:5 .... 26, 27	Rev 17:7 19
Rev 12:1 .... 3, 4, 5, 7	Rev 19:15 29
Rev 12:1 – AT 15	Rev 2:27 29
Rev 12:1-2 9	Rom 10:4 33
Rev 12:1-4 24	Rom 11:21 10
Rev 12:1-5 1	Rom 16:20 5
Rev 12:2 .... 12, 14, 16, 17	Rom 3:20 32
Rev 12:3 18	Rom 5:10 26
Rev 12:4 .... 21, 22, 23	Rom 7:20-23 37
Rev 12:5 26	Rom 8:29 11
Rev 17:3 20	Rom 9:27 12

ABOUT THE AUTHOR

Sheila R. Vitale is the Spiritual Leader, Founding Teacher, and Pastor of *Living Epistles Ministries (LEM)*. She moves in the offices of Teacher of Apostolic Doctrine, Prophet, Evangelist and Pastor, has an international following, and has been expounding on the Scripture through a unique spiritual lens for nearly three decades.

She has written more than 50 books based on the Old and New Testaments including *Ephraim, Man of the Earth and The Eagle Ascended (OT), and Salvation* and *Not Without Blood (NT)*. She has also rendered original spiritual interpretations of Biblical texts such as *The Woman in The Well (John, Chapter 4)* and *First Corinthians, Chapter 11*. Her unique, Multi-Part Message style is seen in *LEM* Serial Messages such as *A Place Teeming With Life* (9 Parts) and *Quantum Mechanics in Creation* (18 Parts). Each Part of a Multi-Part Message Series can also be enjoyed as a complete and independent study. In addition, she has defined, explained, illustrated and demonstrated hundreds of spiritual principles throughout more than 1,000 *LEM* Lectures.

Her signature work, however, is the three volumes of *The Alternate Translation Bible (ATB)*: *The Alternate Translation of The Old Testament, The Alternate Translation of The New Testament* and *The Alternate Translation of the Book of Revelation*. *The Alternate Translation Bible* is a work in progress (*The ATB Project*). Accordingly, additional spiritual interpretations of both whole and partial Chapters are added from time to time, as they are rendered. The most up-to-date versions of *The ATB Project* may be found online at *The LEM* W*ebsite* (*LivingEpistles.org*). *The ATB* is a *spiritual interpretation* of the Scripture and is not intended to replace traditional translations.

She also analyzed the Greek text of *The Book of Revelation* and preached extensively on it in the early years of *The ATB Project*. During that time she produced 197 distinct *Message Parts*, under 29 specific *Message Titles*, all of which deal with *The Book of*

Revelation. Also, many of her books such as, *Adam and The Two Judgments* and *A Study in Unconscious Mind Control*, have been translated into Spanish, as well as *The Book of Revelation*.

Pastor Vitale is an illustrator of spiritual principles, a researcher, a translator and a reviewer of the Modern Social Trends of Family and Culture, as they are revealed through TV programs (*The Sopranos*), movies (*The Matrix* and *The Edge of Tomorrow*) and plays (*Wicked*). She also writes for the *LEM Blog*.

She travels domestically, as well as internationally, preaching and teaching Judeo-Christian Spiritual Philosophy, and has donated Audio Libraries of her Lectures to other ministries in Africa, Asia, Europe and North America,

Pastor Vitale serves *LEM* in a range of spiritual, educational, and administrative functions from *The Selden Centre*, *LEM* headquarters in Selden, New York. She is also a philanthropic individual who supports the *Lighthouse Mission (Patchogue, NY) and HGM – Mission of Hope – Haiti, and other* charitable organizations. She also supports community services such as the *Terryville Fire Department*.

In her spare time, Pastor Vitale enjoys watching movies, attending plays and partaking of cuisines from different cultures. An avid traveler, she has visited several countries in Europe and Africa as well as many cities in the United States.

BEGINNINGS, INSPIRATION AND CALLING

Pastor Vitale began her spiritual journey as a child when her Jewish mother enrolled her in the Hebrew school of an Orthodox synagogue. She experienced the Spirit of God for the first time there in such a profound way that she wept. But after that, when she was only eleven years old, she became very ill and was taken to Mount Sinai Hospital in New York City. She almost died there and has battled with life-threatening health issues ever since. Nevertheless, a deep longing for God continued to pursue her until several years later when she desperately wanted to attend Yeshiva (Jewish high school), but could not. Her secular parents approved of her choice, but could not afford the tuition.

Much later, after years of searching, she once again experienced the Spirit that had brought her to tears in the synagogue of her youth, but this time it was at *Gospel Revivals Ministries*, a Pentecostal church where Deliverance Ministry was emphasized. She had a desire to understand the Bible since she was a child, but Scripture was difficult for her and she struggled with the text. Nevertheless, she read one Chapter of the Bible every day until, one day, *her spiritual eyes opened* and she saw an angel holding a little book.

After that, she attended as many as five teaching services each week for about seven years, the latter part of which she edited *Pastor Holzhauser's* books. But several more years had to pass before *the eyes of her understanding opened even further* and she began to receive *Revelation Knowledge of the Scripture*. She understood at that time that the angel she had seen was the angel of Revelation 10:8.

After about seven years of learning *Deliverance Ministry* and *The Doctrine of Sonship* (*Bill Britton*) from *Pastor Holzhauser,* she studied the Bible independently under the influence and direction of the Holy Spirit.

In **1998** she began teaching Apostolic Doctrine.

In **1990** she spent three months in Stony Brook Hospital where she recovered from an incurable disease, defeating premature death, once again, and went on to resume teaching and managing *LEM*.

In **1992** she journeyed to Africa for the first time, where she was called to the office of Evangelist.

In the **mid-1990s,** she began to Pastor in addition to being a Teacher of Apostolic Doctrine, a Prophet and an Evangelist, thus, satisfying all five offices of *The Ministry of the Lord Jesus Christ to His Church.*

LIVING EPISTLES MINISTRIES

Pastor Vitale was happy fellowshipping at *Gospel Revivals Ministries* but, eventually, she desired a deeper and more spiritual understanding of the Word of God. One day, after crying out to Jesus about her need, she was amazed to hear Him ask her if she would teach. Her initial response was that she did not see how it would be possible since she was already working a full-time job, despite her poor health. But after the Lord asked her for a second and then a third time, she reluctantly agreed, believing that He would empower her to do the job. Shortly thereafter, in the latter part of 1987, she began to teach her own brand of Judeo-Christian Spiritual Philosophy.

The Lord Jesus Christ named the work *Living Epistles Ministries* in 1988.

The first *LEM* meetings were casual and spontaneous gatherings of friends and fellow deliverance workers in Pastor Vitale's home. After that, they were held in the business office of one of the brethren. Pastor Vitale delivered her first formal message entitled *The Truth About Witchcraft in January of 1988*, followed by *The Seduction of Eve* in April of the same year. After that, she prepared and taught weekly messages including *Signs of Apostleship* and *Lazarus & The Rich Man. The meetings eventually* increased to two and then three each week.

Sometime after that, she learned that the Lord Jesus Christ was revealing spiritual principles from the Hebrew text of the Old Testament through her teachings, and she used those spiritual principles to begin to unlock the mysteries of the New Testament, as well. Today she understands that the Scripture is a spiritual document that must be spiritually discerned if it is to be understood correctly, and calls that spiritual understanding **The Doctrine of Christ**.

LEM publishes a wide range of material, including books, e-books, spiritual interpretations of the Scripture and transcripts of many of Pastor Vitale's Lectures and on-line meetings, all of which, as well as the entire *Alternate Translation Bible,* may be viewed free of charge on the *LEM* website (*LivingEpistles.org*). She also has an *Author's Website* where all of her books, as well as several photographs of herself and a short biography are displayed (Amazon.com/author/SheilaVitale). Paperback and digital versions of *LEM* books may be purchased through *Amazon, Google Books* and *Barnes & Noble*.

LEM provides free video livestreams through YouTube and other Internet Platforms . . .

@LivingEpistlesMinistries (2016 – Sept. 2022)
@LivingEpistlesMinistriesLEM (Oct. 2022 – Ongoing)
@LivingEpistlesMinistries (LEM disciples)

. . . as well as two channels of **Shortclips** where short, focused messages of about 15 minutes each are posted:

@shortclipsbysheilar.vitale3334 (2016 – Sept. 2022)
@ShortClips-SheilaVitale (Oct. 2022 – Ongoing)

LEM donates a significant percentage of its income to other Christian ministries and organizations that advocate for Christian values and defend the United States Constitution.

PASTOR VITALE TODAY

Today Pastor Vitale continues to dedicate her life to teaching the spiritual principles of the Bible and focuses daily on studying, writing and preaching powerful messages from *The Selden Centre,* LEM/CCK's headquarters at Selden, New York.

Living Epistles Ministries
Sheila R. Vitale
Pastor, Teacher & Founder
Judeo-Christian Spiritual Philosophy
PO Box 562, Port Jefferson Station, New York 11776, USA
LivingEpistles.org
or
Books@LivingEpistles.org

www.ingramcontent.com/pod-product-compliance
Lightning Source LLC
Chambersburg PA
CBHW070106100426
42743CB00012B/2660